ELECTRIC LOCOMOTIVES OF THE WORLD

ELECTRIC LOCOMOTIVES
OF THE WORLD

F. J. G. HAUT

D. BRADFORD BARTON LIMITED

Frontispiece: The Co–Co Series E50 is characteristic of the new post-war generation of German electric locomotives. They have a weight of 124 tonnes; their six motors give an hourly output of 4500 kw at 79 km/h. Starting tractive effort is 45,000 kg and maximum speed 100 km/h. Germany has also developed multi-current locomotives of various types, notably the Series E410 which can, like the French designs, run under all four main European current systems.

 © copyright D. Bradford Barton 1977   773/3 NB   ISBN 0 85153 256 X

printed in Great Britain by H. E. Warne Ltd, London and St. Austell

for the publishers

D. BRADFORD BARTON LTD · Trethellan House · Truro · Cornwall · England

introduction

When the steam locomotive was invented and put on rails, it may be said to have opened the industrial age. Actually the two did not coincide, as railways or 'tramways' had existed since the Middle Ages, moving goods by horse, cable or weight, while the steam engine started life as a steam wagon on the road. Trevithick, Blenkinsop and others had the idea to put the steam engine on wheels and make it a source of motive power. The Stephensons were the ones who did not invent either the railway or the steam locomotive, but made it a practical working proposition.

The electric locomotive is almost as old as this, as the earliest experiments known to have taken place were in 1835, when two Dutch engineers drove a fourwheeled vehicle by battery power. At the same time, Thomas Davenport of Vermont, U.S.A., tried a similar experiment; all were abandoned for lack of a suitably working electric motor.

The first true electric locomotive was built by a Scotsman, Robert Davidson and employed on the Glasgow-Edinburgh line in 1842. This machine weighed 7 tons and had two axles, hauling a load of 6 tons at 4 mph. All that is known of this remarkable design is that a kind of electro-magnetic system produced current and rotation. The inventor found no support however and the work was not carried on. From 1835 to 1880 many experiments followed both in Europe and U.S.A. but all without practical results. The success that came by 1880 was largely due to the growing electrical industry which sought an outlet for its products, and this suggested railway electrification. The railway companies were not really interested until they encountered problems which the steam locomotive could not overcome; to climb mountains and go through long tunnels, and for suburban traffic moving the ever-growing populations of the large towns where steam railways created serious smoke nuisance and pollution.

The first electric railways appeared with very clumsily designed locomotives which only gradually were improved and refined. It took many years to realise that an electric railway is not only cleaner, simpler, safer and cheaper than that operated by steam but that it also can utilise almost unlimited amounts of power. Steam locomotives, however graceful and cleverly designed, rarely reached a sustained power output of more than 2,000 hp, whilst electric locomotives are in use today of up to 20,000 hp! This is really what killed steam traction – the limitations of its available power to cope with the ever-increasing demand for higher speeds and greater tractive effort. Electrification has to come on railways to give an answer to the aeroplane and it is interesting to note that since the introduction of 'Inter-city' services on British Railways, as well as the similar TEE services on the Continent, internal flights have either been severely curtailed or given up altogether.

The story of the electric locomotive is told in this volume in a few pictures – a difficult task as there have been built (and/or still exist) some 20-25,000 in use throughout the world. The task of selecting a hundred or so examples out of this vast reservoir is quite a daunting one.

The modern electric locomotive is one of the highlights of engineering today. It has not the fascination and charm of its steam sister, and will never have, but it is really a far 'cleverer' machine – the cleverness is hidden behind a smooth exterior. Thus, it needs more study and patience, but the lover of railways will doubtless, in time, come to accept the new girl, because without her there might be no railways at all.

Electric locomotives are shown by their axle arrangements, rather than by wheel arrangements; thus an English 4-6-2 becomes 2-C-1. The 'o' behind a driving axle indicates individual axle drive; the '+' coupled axles or bogies. The rod-drive with coupling rods was intended for steam engines and proved unsuitable for electric traction because of its rigidity, which resulted in fractures of rods, etc. Individual axle drive, invented by the American engineer F.J. Sprague, is either 'nose-suspended' or 'axle-hung' without any flexible means which is good enough for slow speeds and small motors. When larger forces have to be transmitted from motor to axle – in the latest Swiss design 2000 hp per axle – very complex flexible 'drives' or transmission systems are used which employ mechanical, spring, or rubber devices to transmit power by flexible media. These form what is probably the technically most interesting part of the electric locomotive. Basically, an electric locomotive consists of two parts, mechanical and electrical. The former comprises the wheels, axles, power transmission device, frames, bogies and superstructures. The electrical part consists of the 'pantograph', a spring-loaded device to take current from the overhead line or 'pick-up' shoes to take current from a power rail. The current then goes via a protecting main switch to a transformer, and possibly to a rectifier in the case of dc motors. This supplies current in 'steps' to give varying speeds, or in the case of dc systems resistances are cut in and out. Finally, the electrical system consists of the electric motors. The design of the latter followed the fashions of the electrical industry and here it is not possible to describe the various types of motors used. In addition, of course, there are control systems including recently complex electronic programming devices for making driving the locomotive safer and easier.

GREAT BRITAIN

England was among the early countries to electrify some of its railway lines, especially suburban services and some lines for special purposes. Indeed, several of these are unique in still running after 90 to 100 years like the coastal railway in Brighton (designed by Magnus Volk) and the only 'Fell' railway left in the world, climbing Snaefell mountain in the Isle of Man. England also has the largest electrified suburban system in the world, the Southern Region of British Rail. But all these make little use of locomotives and have therefore to be left out of a history of the electric locomotive.

It may surprise many to hear that England planned an early electrification of the section Newcastle-York of the old North Eastern Railway. The latter had as Chief Mechanical Engineer, Sir Vincent Raven; he was perhaps born 30 or 40 years too early, as in the 1920s England had an abundance of cheap coal and few were deeply interested in railway electrification. Raven first electrified the line from Newport to Shildon, (eighteen miles apart and with fifty track miles). 1500 volts direct current was used and ten Bo–Bo locomotives were built. Raven later produced a 2–Co–2 express passenger locomotive which was far ahead of its time. This weighed 102 tons and had six twin-motors of 300 hp output each, transmitting this power through 'quill' drives. However this 1800 hp locomotive, capable of hauling a 460-ton train up 1 in 103 at 42 mph, was little used and after a period in store was scrapped.

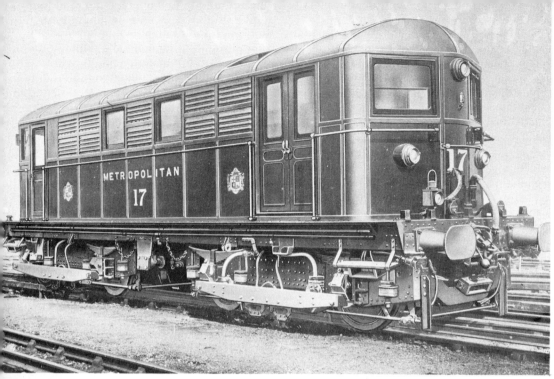

For many years the principal user of electric locomotives in England was the Metropolitan railway; this line received two batches of ten each, in 1904 and 1908, the first series had a central cab and the second, as seen here, had a uniform box structure. All these locomotives were re-built by Metropolitan Vickers in 1922. They were of Bo–Bo wheel arrangement, each axle carrying a 300 hp motor and total weight came out at 61.5 tons; maximum t.e. was 22,600 lbs. Current was collected by four shoes from the 560 v dc third and fourth rail.

In the 1930s, the LNER decided to electrify its 'mountain' section across the Pennines from Manchester to Sheffield. Two locomotive types were designed by Sir Nigel Gresley, a Bo–Bo and a Co–Co. 58 units of the first numbered EM1, were ordered. The prototype was completed in 1941 and after the War was tested in Holland (also electrified with 1500 v dc) where it ran satisfactorily over 200,000 miles. Capable of hauling a 1750-ton train up 1 in 80 it had a maximum speed of 70 mph and weighted 89 tons 18 cwt in working order. Four motors gave a one hour output of 1740/1860 hp and a maximum t.e. of 45,000 lbs.

The Co–Co series of locomotives for the LNER electrification over the Pennines was designed to haul passenger trains, having a maximum speed of 90 mph. They were also built at Gorton Works, with Metropolitan-Vickers (later AEI) supplying the electrical parts. They had a continuous rating of 2298 hp at 46 mph and six motors had a one-hour rating of 2490 hp at 44 mph. They weighed in full working order 102 tons. As the 1500 v electrification was not continued, the locomotives were subsequently sold to Holland. Although satisfactory in service, these locomotives were designed by a steam man and may be said to have been too heavy and out-of-date almost before they started work.

In addition to its vast fleet of underground trains, London Transport also possess nine electric locomotives, used for shunting and maintenance work. These Bo–Bo units work on the same 650 v dc third and fourth rail system and were delivered in 1937/8; weight is 53.8/56.4 tons and the output per one hour 600 hp with a maximum t.e. of 17,800 lbs. They are unique designs, being for use underground.

An unusual locomotive type developed by the Southern Railway for mixed traffic duties appeared in 1943. These three Co–Co locomotives took current from the conductor rail but were also equipped with pantographs for overhead-line working in sidings. Each differs considerably in design but they share the following technical details: weight in working order, 103-105 tons; number of motors six; output for one hour 1470 hp; maximum t.e. 45,000 lbs. An unusual feature is a booster motor control with flywheel to overcome the danger of stalling if there are gaps in the conductor rail system – as occurs at station ends, when the maximum starting effort is required. The SR 750 v dc system is now old-fashioned but is simple and works well. It still serves the main purpose for which it was designed, the South London commuter services, bringing about one million people a day to and from work. The difficulty is the movement of goods on such a low-voltage current rail system and this design is an attempt to solve this problem. To modernise the whole Southern Region and electrify with a high-voltage system would not only seriously interrupt the life and activities of many people but would cost an astronomical sum.

After the formation of British Railways in 1948, the earlier experiments made by the SR were used as a basis on which to order twenty-four Bo–Bo locomotives for the Kent-coast electrification. These are equipped with pick-up shoes as well as pantographs for work in sidings and are mainly used on the Continental train-ferry services. Built at Doncaster, with English Electric supplying the electrical equipment they have four nose-suspended motors and Brown Boveri flexible drive, the one-hour output being 2552 hp. Maximum speed is 90 mph and they work freight trains of up to 900 tons weight; total weight is 77 tons.

In 1958, the British Transport Commission decided to phase out the 1500 v dc system and use as standard for future electrification of British Railways the 25,000 v single-phase alternating current system with industrial frequency (50 cycles), thus following the highly successful French practice. A total of ninety Bo–Bo locomotives was ordered in the first instance from various manufacturers, consisting of types A and B. Seen here is No E 3001 of Type AL1. These locomotives use various forms of power transmission (Alsthom and Brown Boveri); continuous output is 3000 hp with a maximum t.e. of 50,000 lbs. Maximum speed is 100 mph.

A second generation of a similar type for British Railways was series AL6, illustrated here, also with Bo–Bo wheel arrangement. These weigh 81 tons and the continuous output is 3600 hp with a starting power of 6000 hp. These locomotives have one pantograph only – of the modern scissor type. A further batch of thirty-six locomotives, Class 87 (and 86), for the Inter-city services between London-Birmingham-Manchester-Liverpool-Glasgow, are geared for 176 km/h operation, have a continuous rating of 5000 hp, and like the earlier series are also of Bo–Bo wheel arrangement. Weight is 80 tons, and the starting t.e. 42,500 lbs.

FRANCE

Although France has a smaller population than England, it is considerably bigger in size, extending from the Low Countries to the Alps and the Pyrenées. Having ample resources of water power, as well as coal, and with many mountainous lines, it was an early candidate for electrification. The destruction caused during World War II gave a chance to rebuild almost the entire railway system and French engineers developed the locomotive building industry in their country into the leading one in the world. This achievement brought in large export orders, including even Russian and Chinese contracts.

One of the first high-tension locomotives ever built was designed by the Swiss firm of Sécheron in Geneva for the difficult section from St. George-de-Commiers to La Mûre on the French State Railways, using 2400 v dc. The first batch of five Bo–Bo locomotives were delivered in 1903 and had an output of 500 hp, weight 50 tonnes. The metre-gauge line is 30 km long with gradients of up to 1 in 38. In 1931, five further locomotives were delivered by the same firm, with an output of 920 hp.

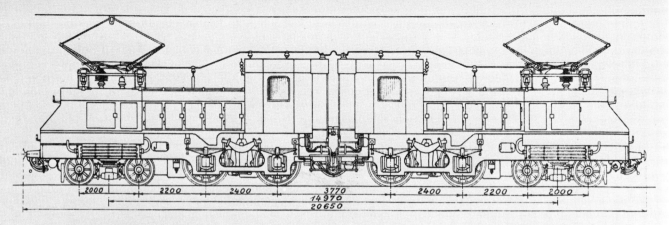

In 1910-11, two French engineers working for the famous engineering firm of Alioth and Schneider designed a single-phase ac/dc locomotive which was supplied to the PLM Railway of France. Several others were built to the same 2–Bo + Bo–2 wheel arrangements, all having vertical traction motors; they weighed 136 tonnes. The four motors had an output of 1800 hp one-hour and used single-phase ac of 1200 v and 25 cycles. Although they were successful, it is not known why the experiments were discontinued.

The former Midi Railway in France ran one of its main lines across the Pyrenées mountains; from 1902 to 1908 they carried out tests to examine whether electric traction could be used for the heavy gradients involved over this line. 1200 v single-phase ac of 16⅔ cycles was decided upon and six different locomotives, all of 1–C–1 layout were ordered from different makers – this order being an important step in the history of electric locomotives. No.3501, supplied by Schneider, was a rod-driven machine which had two motors of 700 hp each and weighed 82 tonnes. As the outcome of the tests, eight 2–Co–2 locomotives were subsequently ordered but these proved unsatisfactory in service and were then re-built for 1500 v dc.

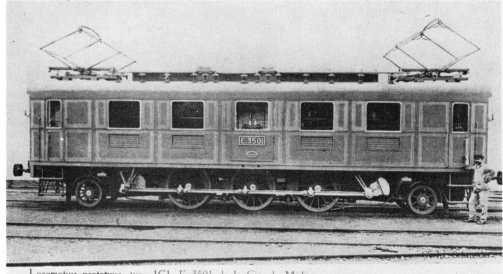

Locomotive prototype, type 1C1, E 3501 de la Cie du Midi

For use on its heavily graded lines, the PLM Railway purchased a number of simple and sturdy locomotives in 1925 which gave very good service. These had the unusual wheel-arrangement 1–A–B+B–A–1 (Bissel trucks) and could use regenerative braking when running down grade. Of 2280 hp, they weighed 122 tonnes and could haul an 800-tonne train up 1 in 66 at 85 km/h. They were long-lived and some remained until 1970, including Series 262 AE 2, a 4000 hp 2–Co+Co–2 locomotive, supplied by Batignolles-Oerlikon.

On the main line from Paris to Orleans, electrified with 1500 v dc, various experiments were tried with locomotives supplied by American firms. Later a most successful design was developed, a 2–Do–2 with Buchli drive. These locomotives weighed 135 tonnes and gave 4950 hp/one hour output at 96.5 km/h. In their original state, before rebuilding in the 1960s, they reached 170 km/h with a 180 tonne train and on test in 1938 one reached even 190 km/h. They are of an unusual layout in having three motors, each of which drives two groups of driving axles through a pair of coupled gear wheels, with intermediate gears and flexible couplings. It was claimed that this arrangement considerably increased the tractive effort compared to individual axle drive. This feature however was not repeated as the complicated drive was costly and difficult to maintain.

Before the Second World War, the SNCF required a heavy locomotive for hauling 1200-tonne trains at 45 km/h on 1 in 100 gradients. A series of experimental locomotives followed which formed the basis of extremely successful designs all of which have Co–Co or Bo–Bo–Bo wheel arrangements. Typical is series CC 6001 with a single body resting on two three-axle bogies, the latter carrying the buffing and drawing gear. Construction was all-welded and the electrical layout was unusual in that the six motors could work either all in series, or in two parallel groups of three in series, or alternatively in three parallel groups of two in series. Rated at 3600 hp these machines weighed 120 tonnes and had a maximum speed of 105 km/h.

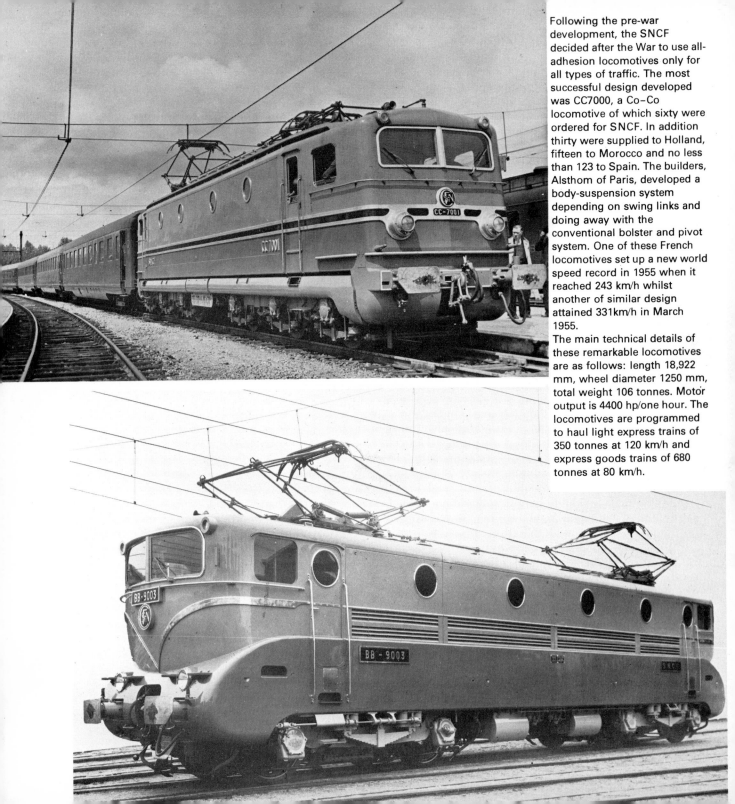

Following the pre-war development, the SNCF decided after the War to use all-adhesion locomotives only for all types of traffic. The most successful design developed was CC7000, a Co–Co locomotive of which sixty were ordered for SNCF. In addition thirty were supplied to Holland, fifteen to Morocco and no less than 123 to Spain. The builders, Alsthom of Paris, developed a body-suspension system depending on swing links and doing away with the conventional bolster and pivot system. One of these French locomotives set up a new world speed record in 1955 when it reached 243 km/h whilst another of similar design attained 331km/h in March 1955.

The main technical details of these remarkable locomotives are as follows: length 18,922 mm, wheel diameter 1250 mm, total weight 106 tonnes. Motor output is 4400 hp/one hour. The locomotives are programmed to haul light express trains of 350 tonnes at 120 km/h and express goods trains of 680 tonnes at 80 km/h.

After the War and the International Railway Congress in London in 1954, the French decided, following the highly successful Hungarian and German experiments to use for all further main-line electrifications the single-phase ac system using 25,000 v and 50 cycles frequency. They equipped a test-line between Aix-les-Bains and La Roche-sur-Foron, 77.6km distant, with gradients of up to 1 in 50. To study the electrical problems involved, test locomotive CC6051, later numbered CC20001, was ordered. The Co–Co locomotive could work both on the test line as well as under 1500 v dc. Following the success of these tests the important line from La Roche-sur-Foron to Thionville was electrified and four different experimental locomotives ordered.

Series BB9003/4, another successful 1500 v design, were ordered from French and Swiss manufacturers; one of these locomotives reached exactly the same speed on tests as the one previously mentioned, namely 331 km/h. The carefully designed locomotives were divided into three masses: (1) the un-sprung parts (wheels and axles), (2) the bogies carried on the primary springing, (3) the body, carried on the secondary springing. Continuous output of the four motors is 4450 hp; maximum speed is 140 km/h. Weight is 80 tonnes, whereby the spring-borne part (body) is 37 tonnes, the spring-borne part (bogies) two × fifteen tonnes = 30 tonnes and the unsprung part is four × three and a quarter tonnes = 13 tonnes.

The above-mentioned 302 km-long line forms an important link in European traffic carrying very heavy and fast passenger and goods traffic, including 1750-tonnes coal and iron trains for the steel works of France and Belgium and the Sarre district as well as twenty/thirty express goods trains per day. On one day 92 goods trains with an average weight of 1140 tonnes used the line. The locomotives ordered were to test 'direct' motors with 'Ignitron' rectifiers or heavier types converting the single-phase ac into dc or three-phase ac on the locomotive. Deliveries were made in 1954. One of these pioneering locomotives, number BB 12000, had the following main dimensions: wheel arrangement is Bo–Bo; total length 15,200 mm; wheel diameter 1250 mm; the weight in working order is 84 tonnes. Total output is 3360/4000 hp and maximum speed 120km/h. The designer was the French firm of MTE.

The next main line to be electrified, from Paris to Lille, was to use the 50 cycle system. In addition to further orders of the test locomotives CC 14000 and BB 12000, two new classes were supplied: BB 16000 and BB 16500. Of the latter, 205 units were ordered from the French firm of Alsthom. The main point of this engine is that it has only one motor per bogie, which drives via intermediate gears a double set of pinions giving two speeds: 150 km/h for passenger work or 90 km/h for freight work. Several quite revolutionary ideas were incorporated, such as a very short bogie of 1608 mm against the usual one of about 3000 mm wheel base. On test the locomotive started a 2410-tonnes train on 1 in 100.

For running under other currents (1500 v dc), the SNCF developed a number of bi-current locomotives; among these was BBB 20003, a 114-tonnes, Bo–Bo–Bo locomotive with three bogies, an hourly output of 3000 hp. Finally followed a series of locomotives which could run under all four of the European current systems, namely: 25,000 v single-phase ac of 50 cycles (France, Gt. Britain); 15,000 v single-phase ac of 16⅔ cycles (Germany, Austria, Switzerland); 1500 v dc (France, Holland) and 3000 v dc (Belgium, Italy).

The four-current Co–Co locomotives, of which CC40101 is one, can run under all the European systems as already mentioned. They have an hourly output of 3850 kw, are 22,030 mm long overall; weight is 107 tonne. The body is mainly made from stainless steel, claiming 20 per cent weight reduction. Each of the three-axled bogies contains only one motor, with double-reduction gear; they can change from one to the other gear-system while travelling. Not only can these locomotives travel under all European current systems; but they are a veritable storehouse of new ideas. Since their appearance a number of designs have copied it and are at present in course of construction.

SWITZERLAND

Switzerland, with its deep valleys, lakes and high mountains, is very difficult terrain indeed to cross and it was, until the arrival of railways, a very poor country. For much of each year the roads were impassable and many communities were cut off in mid-winter. Railways improved all this but when it came to crossing the Alps the Swiss at that date were too poor to undertake such gigantic enterprises themselves and it was largely French and German money which built the Gotthard and Simplon lines and others. As Switzerland has enormous water power reserves, electrification was the obvious answer once it was clear that

electric mountain service was possible. The Swiss electrified all the main lines, becoming entirely independent of imported fuels and also electrified its many smaller lines. Motor coaches are mostly used and thus only two examples are included in this volume. Travel in Switzerland on its spotless trains makes one realise that the fascination of railways comes not only from the steam locomotive but also from the human effort of organisation. The story of Swiss railway electrification is indeed a proud one for all concerned; the men who built and ran the lines as well as the engineers who produced such fine machines. Many of the earliest designs are still in use today after fifty years of uninterrupted service.

The Swiss railways closely followed the progress of the many attempts to use electric traction, as it appeared to them that this form of railway would be ideal for mountain lines with their heavy gradients, many tunnels and severe curves, as well as severe winter weather conditions. In 1899 they electrified a 45 km-long line from Burgdorf to Thun with three-phase current of 750 v. Motor-coaches as well as locomotives were ordered and among these were a –B– and a B–B, seen above. The installation and all vehicles were supplied by Brown Boveri of Baden in Switzerland.

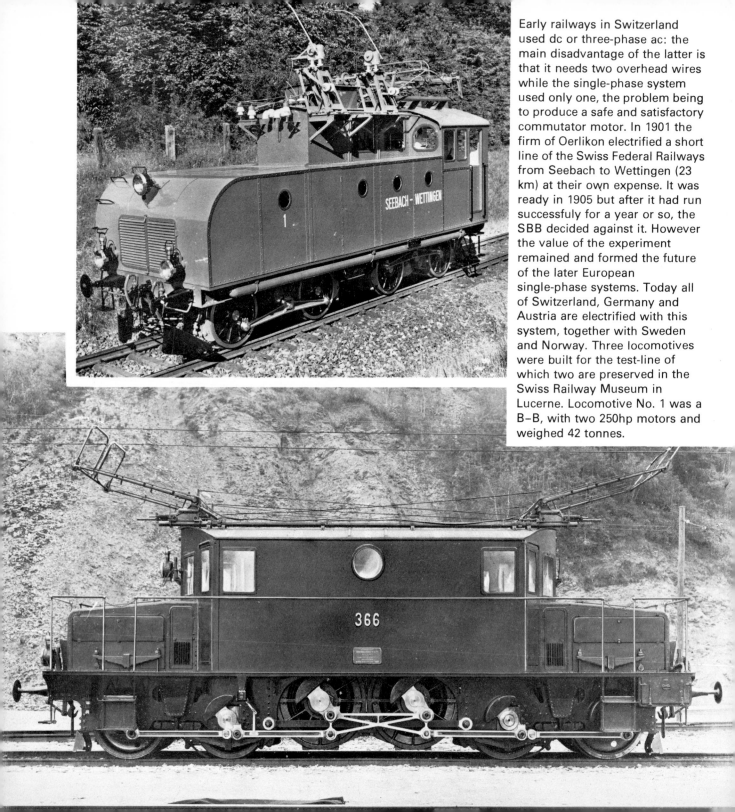

Early railways in Switzerland used dc or three-phase ac: the main disadvantage of the latter is that it needs two overhead wires while the single-phase system used only one, the problem being to produce a safe and satisfactory commutator motor. In 1901 the firm of Oerlikon electrified a short line of the Swiss Federal Railways from Seebach to Wettingen (23 km) at their own expense. It was ready in 1905 but after it had run successfuly for a year or so, the SBB decided against it. However the value of the experiment remained and formed the future of the later European single-phase systems. Today all of Switzerland, Germany and Austria are electrified with this system, together with Sweden and Norway. Three locomotives were built for the test-line of which two are preserved in the Swiss Railway Museum in Lucerne. Locomotive No. 1 was a B–B, with two 250hp motors and weighed 42 tonnes.

The 75 km long Loetschberg line, opened in 1910 with three-phase current, was later changed to the standard Swiss single-phase. The twelve 1–E–1 locomotives used on the line and through the Loetschberg Tunnel (14.6 km long) had 2500 hp output and could work over the 1 in 40 gradients at 50 km/h. Originally, they had two motors, later re-built to four, increasing output to 3000 hp and service speeds to 90 km/h.

The Simplon Pass forms one of the oldest links through the Alps; it was decided to build a railway across it with a tunnel under the summit portion. This 23 km-long tunnel was opened in 1906 and is the longest in the world. The line used electric traction from the outset. Later the Loetschberg line was also built with its own tunnel and the two systems form one of the main links of Europe, connecting Paris, via Berne, with Italy. The Simplon Tunnel rises inside and thus gave serious ventilation problems which forbade the use of steam. Brown-Boveri offered to design suitable locomotives and delivered between 1906 and 1908 a batch of locomotives, 1–C–1 and —D–. The 1700 hp –D– locomotive seen here had 1250 mm wheels, was 11,650 mm in length. It had two speeds of 26 and 52 km/h by using eight and sixteen poles, and also two additional intermediate speeds by using six and twelve poles.

The BLS Railway has always been amongst the foremost in electric locomotive design anywhere in the world. In the 1930s they changed from rod-drive to individual axle-drive and ordered the Series Ae6/8, a 1–Co+Co–1 141 tonne locomotive for express services. In 1944, the Series Ae4/4 was introduced, the first all-adhesion express locomotive ever built. Output per axle was 1000 hp for a weight of 80-tonnes and maximum speeds were possible of 125 km/h. Locomotives of such power needed careful re-designing expecially of the bogies and power transmission, a Brown Boveri flexible disc drive being used. One of the latest designs (1959), is a Bo–Bo+Bo–Bo 8000 hp unit with a starting t.e. of 48,000 kg. This can haul a 900-tonnes train up 1 in 37 at 75 km/h. In 1965 followed series Ae4/4 II, of 80 tonnes weight and with an output of 6240 hp no less than 1500 hp per axle, equalling the previously mentioned 120 tonnes design on six axles. Complex power transfer systems were used to adjust the axle loadings and the locomotives used semi-conductor rectifiers, plus a high-voltage control transformer which feeds in 32 steps the single silicon rectifier and then the four eight-pole series motors.

The Gotthard line is the main railway link between Northern and Southern Europe. Opened in 1882, it is 219 km long (with 46 km in tunnels, including the main one 14 km long). Severe coal shortages during World War I plus increasing train-loads and speeds and the success of the Simplon and Loetschberg electrifications led in 1921 to its electrification with the single-phase ac system of 15,000 v and 16⅔ cycles. Two locomotive designs were developed: a 1–B+B–1 for passenger service with a one hour rating of 2200 hp at 59 km/h and a maximum speed of 75 km/h; weight 106.5 tonnes. Forty of these were built 1918-22. The second design, of which 33 were built, was a goods locomotive, the well-known 'electric iron' type, with 1–C+C–1 wheel arrangement as illustrated above. These had a one hour rating of 2240 hp and weighed 128 tonnes. Various test locomotives were also built, among these No.11000, a 1–Bo–1+1–Bo–1 type, to try out two different motor drives, (Brown Boveri and Tschanz). The latter 133-tonne locomotive (below) was listed as series Ae4/8, No.11000; and had an output of 2650 hp.

After 1940, locomotive design in Switzerland progressed through weight reduction and increased horse-power, mainly by abandoning rod-drive in favour of drive to individual axles. Several very large locomotives were built which worked – and still do – very well but are difficult to utilise fully. The design was 'halved' and two rather less powerful locomotives, series Ae4/6 of 1–Bo+Bo–1 design were developed. Of the large units three were built, Ae8/14 with wheel arrangement 1 – Bo – 1 – Bo – 1 + 1 Bo – 1 – Bo – 1. They appeared in 1931-40 and are 34,000 mm long and have 1610/1350 mm driving wheels. They have either eight or sixteen motors and weigh 246 tonnes with a one hour output of 16,000 hp. The 106 tonne 'half-units' (below) were built in 1941-45 and have eight motors.

Ever-increasing train loads over the Gotthard line necessitated the introduction in 1949 of a six-coupled locomotive series, the Ae 6/6, of 6000 hp output. These weigh 122 tonnes and have six motors. They are capable of hauling 600-tonne loads over the Gotthard gradients of 1 in 37 at 75 km/h and can restart these trains on such gradients, often in very adverse weather conditions.

The newest design to appear is a Series Re 6/6, a Bo–Bo–Bo locomotive again for heavy fast mountain work. They have an hourly output of 10,600 hp at 105 km/h, weigh 122 tonnes and reach a maximum speed of 140 km/h. The design is produced in two different styles, either with a single body or with a twin-articulated layout. This class of locomotive was developed in view of the possibility of building a base-tunnel under the St. Gotthard.

Switzerland possesses numerous small lines which are today entirely electrified and usually serve a number of communities in Alpine valleys. One of them is the metre-gauge Brunig-line of the SBB, which is a combined rack and adhesion line built in 1889-9 between Lucerne and Interlaken. It is 74 km long and since 1941 has used standard single-phase ac of 150000 v and $16\frac{2}{3}$ cycles. Two types of locomotive are used, one being a 'luggage motor van', Series FHe 4/6. These have two cabs and an engine compartment plus space for luggage, parcels and mail. Wheel arrangement is Bo−2−Bo+2z− that is an eight-axle locomotive with four driven axles and in addition two cogwheels; they weigh 57 tonnes and have four motors for work on the adhesion line producing 1215 hp and two motors for the rack section with an output of 1270 hp. Maximum gradient on the line is 1 in 8. Another type of locomotive, Series HGe 4/4, was introduced in the 1960s with the wheel arrangement Bo−Bo+2z and an hourly output of 2180 hp; weight is 54 tonnes.

The Rhaetian Railway is one of the most important narrow-gauge lines in Europe. Of metre-gauge, it uses 11,000 v single-phase ac of 16⅔ cycles although on a number of branch lines dc is used. The line serves the canton of Grison with its famous resorts like Davos and St. Moritz. The 394 km long line has no less than 117 tunnels plus 587 viaducts and bridges, whilst severe winter conditions are experienced; maximum gradients are 1 in 14. Even the line over the Bernina Pass, 2256 metres above sea-level and without a tunnel, is kept open in winter. Since 1921, the line has used powerful locomotives, of which fifteen were supplied and and are still in daily service. Output for one hour is 1200 hp and they have a maximum speed of 45 km/h. The latest type is Series Ge 6/6, a Bo–Bo–Bo with an output of 2400 hp which can haul 250 tonnes up 1 in 28 at 46 km/h. Their weight is 65 tonnes and they consist of two coupled halves carried on three coupled bogies.

GERMANY

Although Germany had some very able engineers and excellent manufacturers, electric traction was viewed with disfavour by the military authorities for many years as it was considered that electric railways were more vulnerable to enemy attack than steam ones – a theory which proved untrue in World War II. However, this hindered serious development in Germany untill the early 1930s when severe unemployment encouraged electrification schemes, whilst later in that decade war preparations by the Hitler regime made fast and efficient transport systems desirable. Thus, large-scale electrification plans were made – as with the autobahns, with an eye to rapid military movements.

The first electric railway in Germany which ran efficiently was the exhibition line 277 m long, built by Werner von Siemens for an exhibition in Berlin in 1879. The locomotive used 150 v current and had three hp output, taking current with sliding shoes from a third rail. It is now preserved in the Technical Museum at Munich.

Between 1899 and 1903 two leading electrical companies (AEG and Siemens) electrified an 8 km-long line and another one of 1.5 km near Berlin using two test cars and two test locomotives on these. The two former reached 216 km/h in 1903 and drew world wide attention to the possibility of electric traction. The line used 10,000 v three phase ac of 25/50 cycles which was transformed down to 1150 or 435 v on the locomotives. The two locomotives weighed 52 tonnes and reached 64 km/h. These experimental lines were regarded as satisfactory but at that time there was little interest in such high-speed travel and the experiments were without immediate consequences. Unfortunately, none of the vehicles was preserved and they are only known through photographs and drawings.

The Prussian State Railways carried out further tests on the Dessau-Bitterfeld line and later electrified the main line from Halle to Leipzig and Magdeburg, and also the so-called Silesian Mountain Railways. The current used was single-phase ac of 10,000 (later 15,000) volts. The locomotives developed were basically copies of then existing steam locomotives. One of these was a 2–B–1 (similar to an Atlantic) with a large single motor mounted in the frame which drove the axles via a disc crank on the armature shaft and a jackshaft with vertical driving rods to the coupling rods. No flexible connection was provided and the design gave trouble with fractured rods. Also designed were 1–D–1 and 1–B+B–1 goods locomotives, with both halves of the latter intended to be used separately. These locomotives were of very unusual design; although they caused difficulties they taught the locomotive designers of the future many basic lessons. Other locomotives ordered were of various arrangements. Seen here is a C+C type, with two driving bogies and four motors positioned in the frame and driving the three coupled axles with jackshafts. An outer frame and Hall's cranks were used as on steam locomotives. The engines had two air-cooled transformers which were mounted at the outer locomotive ends. Although these designs were experimental, they established the 1–C+C–1 and C–C designs, and led to the highly successful German E93 and E94 types plus the French and Swiss Co–Co types already mentioned.

Following the experiments described, the two leading electrical manufacturers in Germany (SSW and AEG) set up a joint 'design bureau' to evolve both efficient passenger as well as goods locomotives. The first to appear was Series E91, a heavy C–C goods locomotive with an hourly rating of 2250 kw at 39.2 km/h and a maximum speed of 55 km/h. After trying rod-drive in a 2–B+B–2 locomotive, the engineers decided this was not really suitable for electric traction and developed the Series E21, a 2–Do–1, of 2840 kw output at 80 km/h and a total weight of 122 tonnes. This design was followed by the highly successful E18, a 1–Do–1 developed in 1934 for heavy fast passenger services at speeds up to 150 km/h. The locomotive has unusual design features, Helmholtz bogies at both ends, all main axles having side play.

For goods and mixed traffic services, Series E44 was developed, a Bo–Bo design of which a total of 188 units were ordered. They weigh 78-82.5 tonnes, and have an output of 1600-2200 kw; maximum speed 80/90 km/h; all are still in service.

For heavy goods services, the AEG-designed E93 was followed by the famous E94 (seen here), a 122-tonne unit of 3300 kw output at 68 km/h, with a maximum speed of 90 km/h. On account of its universal and simple design, this became the German 'electric war locomotive', 145 being built up to 1945 together with a number after the war, plus 44 sent to Austria as war reparations. The design consisted of two bogies coupled together, which carry all traction and buffing gear. Later, German Federal Railways ordered another 142 with more powerful motors (830 kw against 650 kw).

After World War II, Germany was not only divided into two States, but also had to completely reconstruct its railway system. By 1945, of 880 pre-war electric locomotives in service, only half were left and of these only 200 were usable. It was decided to commence a completely new building programme and five test locomotives, Series E10, were ordered in 1950. Also developed was a new Bo–Bo mixed traffic locomotive and a heavy goods locomotive, E50. When tests were complete it was decided to order four different series to meet the ever-increasing demands for higher speeds and output. The Series E10 (illustrated here) had Bo–Bo wheel arrangement, length 15,900/16,100 mm, driving wheel diameter 1250/1350 mm and total weight varies from 80-83.4 tonnes. All had four motors and total output of 3280/3800 kw; maximum speed 130 km/h.

The political division of Germany left two incomplete railway systems which were developed separately. Western Germany followed normal European trends, as already outlined, but Eastern Germany – much the smaller part – also developed electric locomotives but on a much more modest scale. East Germany contains some well-known locomotive works, like AEG-Henningsdorf, now called 'Hans Beimler' People's Own Works. Among the locomotives produced here is Series E11, a Bo–Bo mixed traffic design, also supplied to Poland and Russia. It weighs 82 tonnes and has four motors with a total output of 2800 kw and a maximum speed of 110 km/h with nose-suspended motors, or 140 km/h with flexible power transmission.

In 1963, the German Federal Railways decided to build Series E03, an all-adhesion locomotive designed for 200 km/h speeds of 110
tonnes weight with an hourly output of 6420 kw. The super-structure is no longer a single all-welded self-supporting unit but consists of five sections, each attached to the all-welded frame and connected electrically together, consisting of the two drivers' cabs, two machinery compartments and another long central machinery compartment. The superstructure is all made of aluminium alloys. The bogies are carefully designed for the high speeds intended, tractive and braking forces being transmitted through traction rods to keep axle load changes at a minimum. The drive is by a universal link drive or by a rubber-ring cardan drive. The locomotives weigh 110 tonnes, and have a ten minute-rating of 9000 kw or 12,000 hp; maximum starting tractive effort is 32,000 kg and maximum speed 250 km/h.

AUSTRIA

The Austria of today is very similar to Switzerland both in its geographical layout and its mountainous character. Compared to Switzerland however, it possesses natural reserves of raw materials such as iron, oil, etc, as well as ample water power. However it lacks coal, which in the days of the Hapsburg empire was obtained cheaply from its Czech and Polish possessions. After the war, electrification was an obvious answer, also to reduce unemployment. The country's railway system is now entirely electrified and Austria has a thriving locomotive building industry which exports its products all over the world.

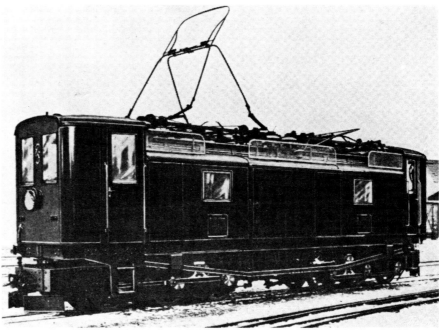

The first railway electrification in Austria was that of a narrow-gauge (760 mm) branch line in Styria in 1911. Ninety-one km long, this rose to an elevation of 632 m, with gradients of up to 1 in 40 across no less than 155 bridges and through 15 tunnels. It was 6500 v single-phase ac of 25 cycles. Eighteen 600 hp C–C locomotives were ordered and are still in use, as seen here, although having been 're-styled' recently.

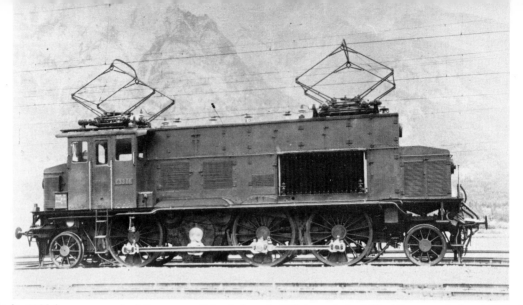

When Austria in 1938 became part of Germany, it had already 650 km of electrified lines and about 250 electric locomotives in service. After World War II, the whole of the Austrian main line system was electrified. Early electric locomotives in Austria followed steam locomotive practice, a 1--C-1 Series 1029, for express services and an -E- Series 1180, for goods trains. Although these were of primitive design, they worked well in service. A 1-C+C-1 was also designed, following Swiss examples. The 1-C-1 and -E- have the following leading details: Series 1029 (later 1073) has an output of 1420 hp, 75 km/h maximum speed and two motors. The -E- locomotives have 1390 hp output with three motors and a maximum speed of 50 km/h.

A heavy -D- 980 hp shunting locomotive was also built for use on Austrian railways. This has 40 km/h maximum speed, a single motor and 1140 mm driving wheels with a weight of 54.8 tonnes.

A series of 1–Do–1
express locomotives
was also developed,
in two series: 1570
and 1670. The hourly
output was 2230/3300
hp and a maximum
speed of 85/100 km/h
was reached. Series
1570 had four motors
(Series 1670, eight) in
the form of vertical
twin motors. In spite
of this unusual design,
these were very
successful and are still
in service.

An all-adhesion
Bo–Bo locomotive
developed by the
Austrian firm of Elin in
Vienna. This was built
in many variants,
starting as a 1530 hp
type and reaching
3220 hp in the final
version; weight varied
from 61.2 tonnes to
83.5 tonnes.

In 1927-8, the Austrian Federal Railways ordered two phase-converter locomotives from Ganz in Budapest prior to the decision to standardise on single-phase ac. This pair of test locomotives were interesting designs with rotary phase-converters, supplying two three-phase induction motors. Then, in 1931 appeared what was probably the most remarkable design of the time, a 1–E–1 phase-converter locomotive, Series 1082. In this, the high-tension single-phase ac was reduced in tension in a transformer and then changed to three-phase ac in a rotary converter. The layout was unusual; the rotating machinery was arranged like a boiler giving the appearance of an electrified steam locomotive. The locomotive underwent exhaustive tests and worked for ten years satisfactorily before being scrapped in 1941.

After World War II, all locomotives were intended to be all-adhesion types of Bo–Bo and Co–Co layout; Series 1010 and 1110 have the latter wheel arrangement and an output of 4000 kw/h for a weight of 109.8 tonnes and a maximum speed of 130 km/h.

U.S.A.

Early railway electrification aroused the interest of various American inventors and engineers – including even Henry Ford – and several specific electrification schemes were mooted, for either mountain lines or those with heavy suburban traffic. Gigantic locomotives, of primitive and clumsy design, appeared. Only one large electrification scheme was carried out, by the Pennsylvania Railroad, as US railways never seriously attempted to fight the ever-growing competition of the motor-car, coach and aeroplane, concentrating mainly on their freight traffic. Apart from Siemens in Germany and René Thury in Switzerland, it was the Americans who whole-heartedly supported electric traction and some of their great engineers and inventors laid the foundations of modern electric traction. The most important figure was probably F.J. Sprague who built a line in 1888, using a trolley pole and is the inventor of the multiple-unit system. Another American, Leo Daft, built the first electric main line locomotive for the Saratoga & McGregor Railroad in 1883, the famous 'Ampère'. Thomas Edison also built three electric railways between 1880-1884. The first large-scale electrification was the one of the Baltimore & Ohio Railroad in 1894 which electrified an underground line to reduce the smoke nuisance. This 7 mile-long section used 650 v dc and a rigid overhead conductor line. The Bo–Bo locomotives had four gearless motors, totalling 1080 hp and could haul a 1870 ton train. Similar electrifications in the U.S.A. to reduce the smoke nuisance in tunnels were carried out by the Boston & Maine Railroad in 1911 (Hoosac Tunnel) and the Spokane and Inland Empire Railroad (St. Claire tunnel) in 1908. In 1909 (68.35 miles long with a 2.61 mile tunnel) the Great Northern Railroad route through the Cascade mountains was electrified, using 6600v ac and Bo–Bo locomotives supplied by GEC. These locomotives weighed 104.5 tons and had an output of 1500 hp. Later several American lines electrified either mountain sections or suburban lines with dense traffic.

The New York, Newhaven & Hartford Railroad was the first U.S. main line which used electric traction for heavy passenger haulage, electrifying its New York – Stamford route in 1907, 33 miles distance, together with New York Central Station and its approaches including the 12 mile line to Newhaven. This electrification was carried out with two types of current and voltage, namely 600 v dc and 11,000 v ac single-phase of fifteen cycles; the first was taken from a current rail, the second from an overhead line. Baldwin and Westinghouse supplied 35 Bo–Bo locomotives and later 36 1-Bo+Bo-1 freight locomotives. Later, a larger 1-Co-1+1-Co-1 locomotive followed. The illustration shows one of the Series 076/0111, a 1-Bo+Bo-1 of 1616 hp, weighing 110 tons.

An early dc electrification was carried out by the Chicago, Milwaukee & St. Paul Railroad in 1920 covering 878 track miles over difficult sections in the Rocky Mountains. Current used was 3000 v dc and the whole electrification was carried out by GEC of U.S.A. They supplied 46 very large and powerful locomotives with the unusual wheel arrangements of 1–Bo–Do+Do–Bo–1, and 2–Bo–Bo+Bo–Bo–2. The first type is seen here, 76′ long with 44″ diameter drivers and weighing 321,200 lbs, with an hourly power output of 4020 hp. In 1920, Baldwin-Westinghouse delivered ten 2–Co–1+1–Co–2, 88′ 7″ long, with 68″ driving wheels, weighing 600,000 lbs. With six twin-motors this gave 4680 hp output.

The most important railway electrification scheme in the United States was on the Pennsylvania Railroad. In 1904, the Long Island line was electrified. In 1915 the section from Philadelphia to Paoli followed and then in 1933, New York-Philadelphia was electrified, extended in 1936 to Washington. This was the major electrification scheme in the U.S.A. and nothing more was done until thirty years later. Except on the 600 v dc Long Island line, the PRR used 11,000 v single-phase ac of 25 cycles. Among the locomotives used were 1–B+B–1 types which could collect current either overhead or, in the Hudson River tunnel, from a third rail.

Another early d.c. electrification was one on the Norfolk & Western Railroad (29.83 miles long) on the Elkhorn tunnel line. Westinghouse supplied 1–B–B–1+1–B–B–1 locomotives with phase-converters turning the 11000 v single-phase 25 cycle line current into three-phase ac on the locomotives. In double tracking two of these locomotives could haul a 3280 ton train at constant speeds of approximately 14 and 28 mph on 1 in 100. In 1926, this electrification was extended to Williamsburg, 112 miles distant and additional locomotives, of the same wheel arrangement, were ordered, weighing 350 tons. These had two motors per unit and an output of 4000 hp.

In 1919 the Pennsylvania Railroad put into service this enormous locomotive, nicknamed 'Big Liz'; a 1–C+C–1 monster with two twin motors driving a jack-shaft and then, via cranks and coupling rods, the driving wheels. It was a single-phase/three-phase converter locomotive with two running speeds only, 11 and 20 mph, 76' 6" long and weighed 499,520 lbs. Power output was 4800 hp. It hauled 3800 ton-trains over the Allegheny Mountains with 1 in 50 gradients and the famous 'Horseshoe Curve'.

As already stated the main U.S. electric railway scheme was the electrification of the main line from New York to Philadelphia and Washington. Used on this was the Class GG1 seen here, a 2–Co+Co–2 passenger locomotive. It was one of the first to be 'streamlined' – or as it was then termed 'air-smoothed'. Designed for speeds of 90 mph or more it was probably the most powerful and advanced design of its day. The motors had a continuous rating of 4620 hp; 139 units were built.

48

In 1951-52 twelve converter locomotives were ordered, among them a Bo–Bo–Bo + Bo–Bo–Bo; they use standard dc motors and have a starting tractive effort of 187,750 lbs! They are rated at 6000 hp having twelve 500 hp motors. In 1962-63, a further 66 Co–Co locomotives were ordered, Series E 44 (below). They weigh 195 tons for an output of 4400 hp. Such a locomotive can haul a 6500 ton train at 33/55 mph. They use rectifiers to provide dc for motors. Maximum speed is 70 mph.

In 1924-25, the Virginian Railroad electrified part of its main line over the 134 miles from Mullens to Roanoke. The railway was mainly a coal carrier and large Mallet steam locomotives worked trains of up to 16,000 tons weight over gradients up to 1 in 50. The electrification scheme was carried out by Westinghouse, its most interesting feature being the 36 enormous triplex locomotives with 1 – B – B – 1 + 1 – B – B – 1 + 1 – B – B – 1 wheel arangement supplied. These had a maximum t.e. of 277,500 lbs. and a 6000-ton train could be moved up-hill and a 9000-ton train downgrade. Current was 11,000 v single-phase ac converted to low-voltage dc on the locomotive. There were only two speeds, 14 and 28 mph; the locomotives, 152′ long, had 62″ driving wheels and an hourly output of 7125 h.p.

Four Bo–Bo–Bo–Bo+Bo–Bo–Bo–Bo units were ordered by the Virginian Railroad, again with ac/dc converters. These giants, one of which is illustrated above, weighed 454 tons and yielded 7800 hp. In 1957, twelve Co–Co 3300 hp locomotives were also supplied by GEC (below). These weigh 197 tons and give 79,500 lbs tractive effort at 15.75 mph. Maximum speed is 65 mph. The illustration of one of these units gives a good impression of the modern electric locomotives now used in the U.S.A.

In 1927-28 a new Cascade tunnel was bored, 7.79 miles long, on the Great Northern Railroad, the longest railway tunnel in America, in conjunction with electrification of 72 miles of this route through the Rockies. Current was changed from three-phase ac to single-phase ac of 11,500 v and 25 cycles. Among the new locomotives was a 1–C+C–1 design of 3300 hp; also ordered were 1–Bo–Bo–1+1–Bo–Bo–1 from Westinghouse and Baldwin. In 1948, Bo–Do+Do–Bo types were delivered by GEC of U.S.A. These have a continuous output of 5000 hp, are 101' long and weigh 320 tons. They have two motor generators of 3000 hp each which drive the two traction generators and exciters per unit. The electrical equipment consists of four dc generators, normally in parallel at low speeds and in series at high speeds; exciters are used for starting the ac motors.

Among the leading railways in the U.S.A. was the New York Central operating route which linked New York, Boston and Chicago. At the height of its prosperity, it possessed 16,000 track miles and carried a large amount of the traffic in New York State. Among the first electrification undertaken by the NYC was the one under the Hudson River where the approaches to the Grand Central Terminal were electrified. This initial electrification comprised 69 route and 360 track miles, using 650 v dc electrification from a side rail. Among the locomotives supplied were Bo–Bo + Bo–Bo and Bo–Bos, all by GEC of U.S.A.

The New York, Newhaven and Hartford Railroad operates 351 track miles and is now using 11,000 v single-phase ac of 25 cycles. Between 1931 and 1943 twenty-six 2–Co + Co–2 locomotives, as seen above, were put into service and were designed to haul 5000-ton trains on level track. They have six twin-motors rated at 800 hp each. In 1954, 174-ton Co–Co rectifier locomotives were supplied, with an output of 4000 hp. No.370 is an example of one of these.

53

Between 1906-09, 47 locomotives of the wheel arrangement 2–Do–2 were delivered for the New York Central Railroad. They had the serial number 'S' and were designed for an hourly output of 1695 hp and a maximum speed of 60 mph.

Russia ordered in 1950 twelve electric locomotives from GEC of U.S.A. suitable for running under 3000 v dc. These 5100 hp locomotives weigh 290 tons and are 89' long. However the export of these engines was forbidden by the U.S. Government and they were bought by the Chicago, Milwaukee and St. Paul Railroad, after altering them from the Russian 5'6" gauge to 4'8½". The popular staff nick-name for these locomotives is 'Little Joes'.

ITALY

The Italians are individualists – and their locomotives, whether steam or diesel or electric, certainly the oddest-looking designs which ever ran on rails. But strangely enough the Italians were not only pioneers but their early three-phase ac two-wire locomotives worked very well despite being of most complex construction; in fact, only recently have the last of them gone after 60-odd years of useful service. Italy needed to electrify early on its routes through the mountains and in 1900-10 the only efficient electric system was the three-phase one. The illustrations show clearly the Italian development which actually started with the ideas of a great genius of electric railway design, a Hungarian, Koloman von Kando; early electrification in the country followed his ideas.

In 1896 Kando built a three-phase locomotive for use on a short test line in Budapest which used 3000 v three-phase ac. As a result, in 1902 the builder, Ganz, received contracts to electrify the Italian Valtellina and Giovi lines with the same current system. Three- and four-axle locomotives were built which were highly successful in spite of their cumbersome appearance and some remained in service into the 1960s. A typical design is shown opposite, built in 1906. The 1–C–1 Series 38 had four motors and was 11,540 mm long with 1560 mm driving wheels. It weighed 62 tonnes, with an output of 1500 hp at 62 km/h and 850 hp at 25 km/h. For the so-called Giovi line (Genoa-Novi), with gradients of 1 in 29, two types of locomotive were developed, the series E 50 freight locomotive and the Series E 30 1–C–1 for passenger service. Each had two motors , of 1000 and 1300 hp respectively. The freight locomotive had two speeds only, 22.5 km and 45 km/h, while the passenger locomotives had four speeds (37.5, 50, 75 and 100 km/h). Weights were 60 and 73 tonnes respectively and output 2000 and 2600 hp. Then followed an –E– locomotive, Series E 551, which weighed 72 tonnes and had a maximum tractive effort of 18,000 kg. Power transmission was either by a triangular coupling rod or by a system of links and rods. Control of the motors was by pole-changing (twelve or eighteen poles) and this class had four speeds (25, 37.5, 50 and 75 km/h).

In the 1920s, the Italian State Railways carried out experiments with 10,000 v three-phase ac of 45 cycles on the Rome-Sulmona line to compare this system with other experiments with 3000 v dc on the Benevento-Foggia line. Among the test locomotives was Series E470, a 1–D–1 1300 hp locomotive with Kando triangular rod-drive and two 930 v changeable-pole motors.

Although the tests mentioned clearly showed the advantages of the three-phase system, it was the twin-wire requirement which led to the adoption of the simpler 3000 v dc system and a gradual changeover to the latter. A system of standardisation was introduced and up to 1967 only six types of dc locomotives were ordered, Series E424, 326, 428, 626, 636 and 646. Standardisation of mechanical parts was very advanced with only four types of driving axle and one design of four-wheel bogie. Electrical equipment was also standardised.

Illustrated here is one of the Bo–Bo–Bo Series E646 in which three independent bogies carry two frames; there are twelve motors driving the axles via spring-loaded ring-drives. They have a one-hour output of 4320 kw and three different transmission systems to allow for maximum speeds of 115-145 km/h.

Series E428 has a one hour output of 4000 hp with eight motors and a
weight of 128 tonnes. Wheel arrangement is 2–Bo–Bo–2.

The first Swedish electric line was built in 1905 near Stockholm and British Westinghouse (later AEI)
supplied a 300 hp, 24-ton locomotive of –B– wheel arrangement for this. Other participants were the
German firms of AEG and Siemens. The tests were highly satisfactory and led to the famous
Ricksgräns-electrification in Lapland, the northernmost line in the world, the main purpose of which was
to expedite year-round exploitation of the huge iron ore mines. Among the early locomotives was the
Series Z, a Bo–2 locomotive built by ASEA in 1910: weight 52 tonnes; 4800 kg maximum t.e.; maximum
speed 75 km/h.

SWEDEN and NORWAY

Ample water power and the unsuitability of steam locomotives in Arctic winter conditions made electrification desirable from an early date on Scandinavian railways. Sweden has only one important electric firm, ASEA of Västeros, a concern which has pioneered many novel ideas. The railway systems in both countries are now 100 per cent electrified.

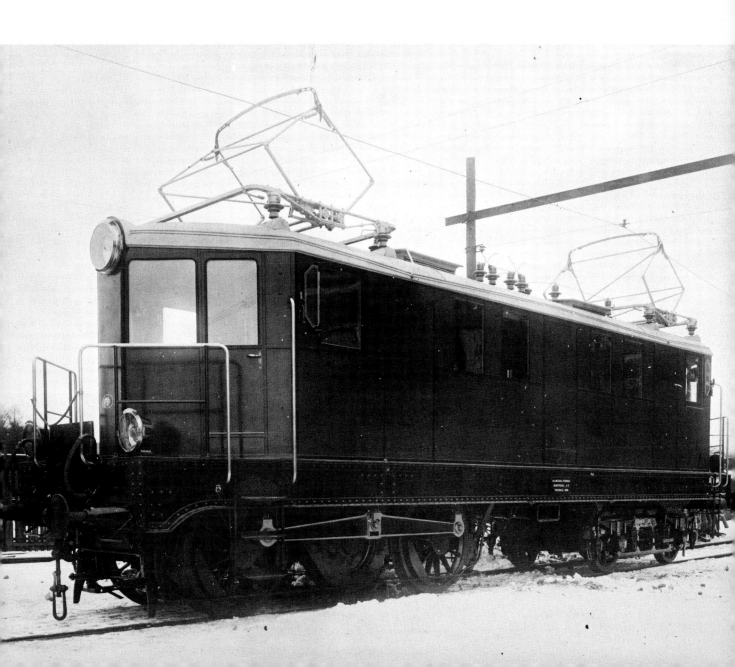

The Swedish State Railways decided in 1920 to electrify the country's main line, 460 km long, between Stockholm and Gothenburg. This work was completed in 1925 with 15,000v single-phase ac of 16⅔ cycles. Firstly 1–Co–1 locomotives were ordered, followed in 1930 by two very advanced types, a 1–Do–1 of Series F, and a Co–Co of Series M. Both these used individual axle drives with hollow shafts. Twenty-four Series F units were delivered (as illustrated here) between 1942-49. They have a maximum speed of 135 km/h, weigh 101.6 tonnes and have four 645 kw motors.

The Ricksgräns (or Frontier) line is 450 km long and runs from Lulea to Narvik, finally linking with the Norwegian section and completed in 1923. The locomotives used were 2–B–2 passenger types, of 1000 hp, and 1–C+C–1 freight locomotives of 1600 hp output; these were delivered between 1911 and 1918. Later, heavier 1–C+C–1 were ordered, as well as a –D– goods locomotive and 2–B+B–2 passenger locomotive. This illustration is one of the 2–B–2 type, built in 1915 (Series Pa) with a maximum speed of 100 km/h and one 665 hp motor; total weight 91 tonnes. Illustrated below is one of the freight types, Series 001 and 06, of which twelve were delivered; maximum speed 60 km/h; two 590 hp motors; weight 125/136 tonnes.

In 1960, the Series DM.3 1–D+D+D–1, entered service, with a maximum speed of 75 km/h and six 950/1200 kw motors. The purpose of these giant locomotives which weigh 258/270 tonnes is the haulage of heavy iron ore trains in the severe conditions of the Arctic winter.

Sweden's railways have been active in developing a modern high-speed all-adhesion locomotive and after tests extending over ten years (between 1948-58) the Series Ra, which have now run over a million kilometres, was ordered in large quantities together with a further experimental series Rb 1–3. One of these Rb types is shown here. Their maximum speed is 120/150 km/h and they have four 825 kw motors; weight varies between 73.6 and 75.2 tonnes. Norway has also an extensive electric railway system including various private lines; the main line locomotives are practically identical with the Swedish ones already described.

These two countries played little role in the history of railway electrification – they have no locomotive building industry of their own of any substance and are too poor to develop or import modern ideas. Thus the electrification schemes have remained piecemeal and have no coherent pattern of development.

The first Spanish electrification was on the Southern Railway between Gergal and St. Fé, 22.7 km long, with 1 in 37 gradients. This was of 1673 mm gauge and was electrified with 5500 v three-phase ac of 25 cycles, the Swiss firm of Brown Boveri carrying out the work. Five –B– locomotives were supplied; they had two three-phase squirrel-cage motors of 160 hp each and in 1923 two more locomotives were supplied with 360 hp motors.

One of the important Spanish main line electrifications was the Orviedo-Leon-Ponferrada section which carries heavy mineral traffic and uses 3000 v dc. The line has 71 tunnels and 156 bridges and rises on grades of 1 in 50 to 1216 m above sea-level. The first six Co–Co locomotives were supplied by GEC of U.S.A. whilst in 1953 English Electric supplied twenty Co–Co – 3600 hp locomotives, including No. 7724. These have a weight of 119.8 tons, six 600 hp motors and a maximum speed of 110 km/h.

Metropolitan-Vickers also supplied a 3600hp 2–Co+Co–2 express locomotive for the same Spanish main line, weighing 150 tons. The French firm of Alsthom have also supplied some very modern all-adhesion locomotives, among them a 3200 hp Co–Co in Series 7600.

One of fifteen Bo–Bo locomotives supplied to Portugal in 1956 by a French group of builders. These locomotives weigh 71 tonnes, have a one hour output of 2176 kw and maximum speed of 120 km/h. The electrification, comprising several lines radiating from Lisbon, was carried out with the French system of 25,000 v single-phase ac of 50 cycles.

RUSSIA

Russia probably has the largest electric railway network in the world. Although it has built up a substantial industry and buys heavily from its satellites – notably East Ger- many, Poland and Czechoslovakia – it is interesting to note that large orders have also been placed in France and Germany. All electric locomotives for Russian service ap- pear to be designed for heavy freight traffic.

Facts are difficult to come by but in 1959 and 1961 substantial orders were placed in France and Germany for heavy locomotives of Series T.01 and TP01, also ten of Series F1 and twenty-five of Series K 07. After a study group had visited the U.S.A. in the late 1930s it was decided to electrify the Transcaucasian and Ural mountain lines, with their steep gradients and heavy mineral traffic. Originally 3000 v dc was used and a typical design of that period is Series VL19 (opposite), a Co–Co locomotive. All these types, built in Great Britain, Italy and U.S.A., have a simple Co–Co layout, nose-suspended motors and an output of 3000 hp; weight is 130/140 tonnes, illustrated here. Also built was a 2–Co–2 express passenger locomotive Series PB21.

Later locomotives ordered were all designed for the French system of 25,000 v single-phase ac of 50 cycles, probably for the complete electrification of the Trans-Siberian railway. These French-built locomotives, as seen opposite, are 23,060 mm long, have 1280 mm wheels and weigh 138 tonnes. With an hourly output of 6300 hp, they are designed for a maximum speed of 75/h and can work in extremes of climate, between +40°C and −50°C. Even larger locomotives have been ordered, also from France, among these a Bo–Bo+Bo–Bo.

Hungary, although only a small country, has played an important role in the history of railway electrification, notably through the firm of Ganz, of Budapest. They were pioneers of three-phase traction and received many international contracts, amongst the most important being the Simplon and Löetschberg electrifications.

For the first Hungarian main line electrification 16,000 v single-phase ac of 50 cycles, twenty-nine 1–D–1 and three –F– locomotives were ordered, one of the former being shown here. These had 1660 mm driving wheels and maximum speed was 100 km/h.

◁

Built between 1915 and 1920, a Ganz –E– test locomotive, following the ideas of their chief engineer, K. von Kando, for the Simplon electrification. This carried two synchronous rotary phase-converters taking 15,000 v single-phase ac current from the overhead line and transforming it into three-phase ac.

During World War II, two locomotive types were developed in Hungary, following more modern trends and using individual axle drive. Among them was this 2–D–2 of 4000 hp output which was later destroyed in an air raid. Another type introduced was a 3200 hp Bo–Co locomotive with five motors.

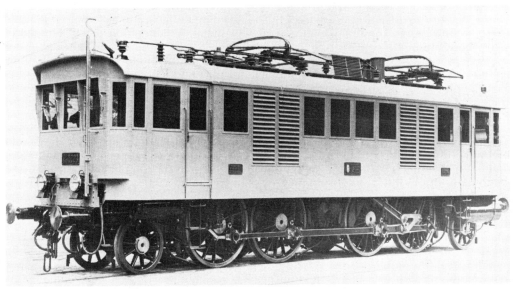

CZECHOSLOVAKIA

This country opened its first electrified line in 1903. Various schemes followed until the great havoc caused by World War II involved a complete reconstruction, when it was decided to electrify all main lines using 3000 v dc.

In 1962, Krupp and AEG supplied Series V43, Bo-Bo locomotives that can run under 16,000 v as well as 25,000 v ac. They weigh 77.5 tonnes and have a continuous output of 2140 kw.

The first electric locomotives in Czechoslovakia ran on the 26 km long line from Tabor to Bechin, opened in 1903. Using 1400 v dc the 29-ton locomotive collected current via 2 × 2 pantographs and had four 130 hp motors. It is now preserved in the Railway Museum at Prague. In 1928 followed the electrification of the main station in Prague and its surrounding lines. Several 1–Do–1 passenger locomotives were ordered from Skoda, Series E466. They had four driving axles, the inner ones being rigid and the outer ones formed with the running axles Krauss bogies. With four twin-motors they had an output of 1900 hp; maximum speed was 110 km/h and the weight 86 tonnes.

This illustration shows one of the Czech post-war designs, Series E499, a mixed traffic Bo–Bo locomotive of 3200 hp. Its maximum speed is 120 km/h.

AUSTRALIA

Australia is too immense and too sparsely populated to have much purpose for costly electric railway schemes and they are thus confined to mountain sections or suburban services. Electrification schemes commenced with the Sydney suburban network in 1926-27, comprising 120 miles worked with 1500 v dc. Electric traction has also been extended to Lithgow over the Blue Mountains. Forty Co–Co locomotives were supplied by AEI which can haul 2200-ton trains double-headed. One of these 108-ton locomotives, which have an hourly output of 1900 hp, is illustrated here.

NEW ZEALAND

New Zealand, having considerable resources of water power, introduced electrification on various of its 3'6" gauge main line routes from the late 1920s onwards. English Electric supplied Bo–Bo 1200 hp locomotives of 1500 v dc. Later, in 1951, a batch of 2–Do–1 locomotives followed, with 1240 hp continuous output; one of which is illustrated below.

One of the recently electrified sections on the South Island is that at Otira for which English Electric supplied a Bo–Bo–Bo series which had notably good riding qualities over the sharp curves. 62′ long, these locomotives weigh 75 tons and have a maximum t.e. of 42,000 lbs.

SOUTH AFRICA

Although small, the industrial belt in the Republic is heavily populated and now has a most efficient and up-to-date electrified railway system, which is almost exclusively a creation of British industry. Main line electrification work started in 1922, including the difficult Pietermaritzburg-Glencoe section, using 3000 v dc. AEI supplied seventy-eight Class 1E locomotives, wheel arrangement Bo–Bo. These were extremely successful and no less than 350 units had been ordered by 1964, as well as 535 sets of electrical equipment to be used for mechanical parts built in RSA. These Bo–Bo locomotives have four 300 hp traction motors and are probably the most numerous class of electrics ever produced. The latest development, Class 5E, weighs 85 tonnes and has a one-hour output of 2100/2290 hp.

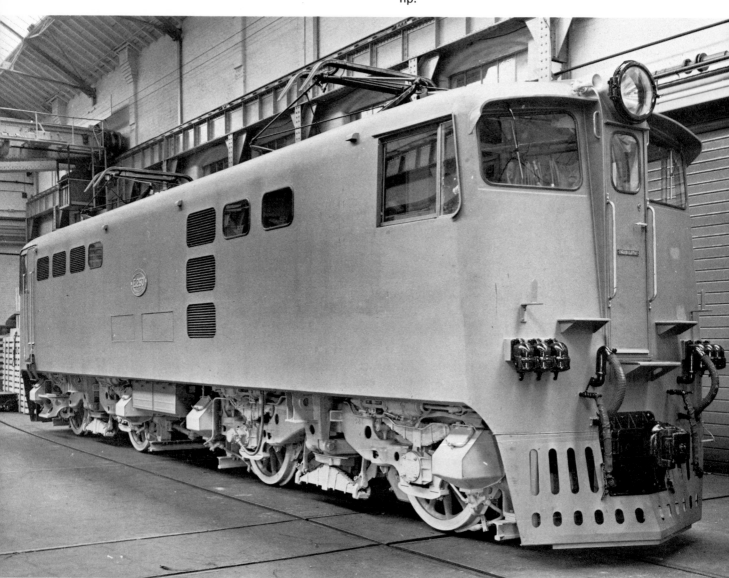

E 1078 and E 1135, photographed at Pietermaritzberg, are a pair of the 2000 h.p. electric locomotives built by Vulcan Foundry Ltd. (part of the English Electric Group) for SAR.

Two of South African Railways earlier electric classes, E 179 and E 183, at Masons Mill depot, Pietermaritzberg, February 1976. SAR have some 1500 electric locomotives in service of which the great majority work in Natal or Western Transvaal where traffic is heaviest.

MEXICO

In Mexico the line from Mexico City to Vera Cruz, 246 miles route, was electrified in 1924. This line reaches 8323' above sea level at one point and has severe (1 in 21) gradients. Current used was 3000 v dc and twelve Bo-Bo-Bo locomotives were supplied by GEC of U.S.A. These locomotives weigh 309,000 lbs and have six nose-suspended motors with a one-hour output of 2736 hp.

HOLLAND and BELGIUM

Both countries faced similar problems in their railway work as England. After the destruction of the War they decided on 100 per cent electrification, retaining the 1500 v and 3000 v dc systems respectively. Holland in particular has a very extensive electrified railway system, using mostly motor-coach trains as in England; the country is electrified with 1500 v dc. After the extensive damage caused during World War II, ten 4500 hp 1–Do–1 locomotives were ordered among others in 1948, based on Swiss designs. These very powerful locomotives were put into universal use being able to haul 2000 tonnes – mineral trains at 60 km/h and 230 tonnes express trains at 160 km/h. The locomotives weigh 100 tonnes and have eight motors and a one-hour output of 4480 hp.

OERLIKON 53262

Later, twenty-five 2900 Co–Co locomotives were ordered which have a maximum speed of 140 km/h. This design follows American practice and the 108 tonne locomotives have a maximum t.e. of 21,000 kg.

Belgium uses 3000 v dc and decided after the War to electrify the whole railway system in the country. A considerable number of locomotives were ordered from various manufacturers, of which Series 123 is characteristic. It has four motors and its one-hour output is 2800 hp. Weight is 93 tonnes; eighty-three units were built between 1955 and 1967.

The 5'6" gauge Great Indian Peninsular Railway was the first in India, opened in 1853. It was also the first railway to use electric traction in 1922 when it electrified the Bombay surburban services, together with the difficult mountain section from Kalgan to Poona and Igatpuri. Current used was 1500 v dc, later converted to 3000 v. Metro-Vic supplied 2610 hp C–C locomotives, the two bogies each carrying two 650 hp motors.

INDIA and PAKISTAN

It is said that the English Colonial Empire left two things in India; the language and the railways. With its ever-increasing population and political situation, the now three times divided country faces problems that appear almost beyond solution. Thus the Indian railway system is neglected and although electrification schemes have been carried out, they have been piecemeal and are of little economic benefit. India would be an ideal country for railway electrification but a great deal of work is required before any full scale electrification could be contemplated.

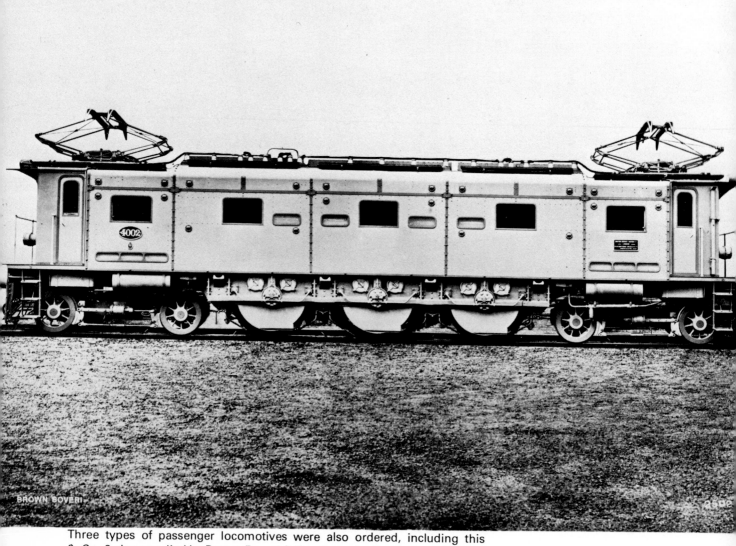

Three types of passenger locomotives were also ordered, including this 2–Co–2 also supplied by Brown-Boveri & Hawthorn, Leslie, having a 2160 hp output from six 360 hp motors.

India has one of the largest railway networks in the world, 48,470 miles of track and 34,180 miles of route. 16,160 miles of broad gauge (5'6") and the rest narrow gauge. Since the last war, substantial electrification schemes have been built including the Calcutta suburban lines and the Durgapur-Benares line using the now-standard single-phase ac of 25,000 v and 50 cycles. By 1967, a considerable number of locomotives had been supplied. Typical of these new designs is Class BBM1 which has to operate in temperatures between 70°C and 0°C. The locomotives weigh 74 tonnes and have a continuous output of 2140 kw.

For the Indian 3000 v dc electrification, British industry supplied several contracts; among these were class EM2, a Co–Co design of 112 tonnes and hourly output of 3120 hp. Maximum speed is 70 mph.

SOUTH AMERICA

The remarks made with reference to Australia apply here too. In addition, most South American countries are beset by political problems which hinder orderly industrial development. Apart from various suburban electrifications in Brazil and the Argentine, there is one of great technical interest, the Transandine Railway of Chile which crosses South America from east to west. It starts in Buenos Aires and goes to Valparaiso in Chile. The mountain section is 249 km long and was opened in 1910. It reaches 3207 metres above sea-level, and has eleven rack sections, the longest being 9 km. Maximum gradients are: on rack 1 in 12.5 and on the adhesion line 1 in 40. There are of course very severe winter conditions. In 1927, the line was electrified, Brown Boveri and SLM-Winterthur supplying rack-and-adhesion locomotives of the type illustrated here. The six driving motors are divided into four groups. Two of these have two motors and are used on the adhesion section; the two inner motors drive cog-wheels. The motors are rated at 235 kw (one-hour). The line uses 3000 v dc. The locomotives weigh 85.6 tonnes and have a maximum speed of 40 km/h on adhesion and 16 km/h on the rack section. In 1957, a further type was ordered, a Bo–Bo with two rack wheels.

JAPAN

Japan has been called the 'England of the Twentieth Century' and the total absence of coal invited electrification once the country became industrialised. It is an important feature that in 30-odd years Japan has built up a substantial electric railway industry which recently has produced some excellent designs and even won export orders. Japan has a large number of electrified lines and an excellent locomotive industry. Electrification started in 1906-12 when two small lines (including that over the Usui pass) were electrified.

In 1922 followed the electrification of the Tokaido line, Tokyo-Kobe, 590 km; it was completed only in 1925 after a catastrophic earthquake. Electrification was difficult because of the 3'6" gauge and the many tunnels. (The new Tokaido line is standard gauge but does not use locomotives.) All lines use dc, varying from 600 to 1200 or 1500 v. In 1922 English Electric supplied a Bo–Bo locomotive of 59 tons weight and 820 hp output as well as a 2–Co+Co–2 express locomotive weighing 100 tons and having 1830 hp output.

After buying its locomotives from abroad, this policy changed in the 1930s. A Japanese locomotive industry developed and has now even entered the export field. At the end of the War, 1875 kms were electrified, all with 1500 v dc, then experiments started with 25,000 v single-phase ac of 50 cycles. Among the first locomotives supplied by the Japanese firms of Mitsubishi and Hitachi was a Bo–Bo+Bo–Bo goods locomotive, Series EH 10, for the original Tokaido line. Hourly output 2500 kw at 49.6 km/h and a maximum speed of 120 km/h. These locomotives, weighing 120 tonnes, first appeared in 1954 and a considerable number have since been built.

Among the 50 cycle ac traction engines a typical example is Series EF 30, a Bo–Bo–Bo locomotive. This is a rectifier locomotive weighing 96 tonnes with an hourly output of 1800 kw and a maximum speed of 110 km/h.

INDEX